CW01072316

To:

From:

ZONDERVAN

*Gratitude*
Copyright © 2009 by Zondervan

Requests for information should be addressed to:
Zondervan, *Grand Rapids, Michigan 49530*

ISBN 978-0-310-82286-8

*Design by Jody Langley*

*Printed in China*

09 10 11 12 13 14 15 • 23 22 21 20 19 18 17 16 15 14 13 12 11 10 9 8 7 6 5 4 3 2 1

Let the word of Christ dwell in you richly as you teach and admonish one another with all wisdom, and as you sing psalms, hymns and spiritual songs with gratitude in your hearts to God.

Colossians 3:16

# CHOKING ON CHOCOLATE

The English playwright J.M. Barrie was at the home of a couple he knew when the woman said to her young son, "Stop eating that candy or you'll be sick tomorrow."

"No," said the boy, as he calmly went on eating, "I shall be sick tonight." Barrie was so struck by the exchange that he put it in his play, Peter Pan. What happened to the boy remains a mystery.

People who have every appetite gratified from childhood on become the least capable of gratitude. To become grateful, we must learn that we can handle disappointment and delayed gratification with grace and perseverance. This is why practices such as fasting and simplicity are such powerful tools for transformation. The experience of frustration and disappointment is irreplaceable in the development of a grateful heart.

John Ortberg

# AN ICE CHEST WILL DO

What is a particular object worth? The only real answer is "whatever someone is willing to pay."

Although taste is often associated with the arts, we also have tastes in people, places, activities, food and practical things like refrigerators. A new refrigerator might cost as little as five hundred dollars or as much as several thousand dollars. Do you need a three-thousand-dollar refrigerator? Do you even want one? If so, why? Many people get trapped into buying more expensive items under the delusion that they are buying higher quality, but really, what do we want our refrigerators to do? We could ask a similar question about every item we buy. Ask God to teach us to correctly appraise the treasures of our lives.

David and Lo-Ann Trembley

Clothe yourselves with the Lord Jesus Christ, and do not think about how to gratify the desires of the sinful nature.

Romans 13:14

*Give thanks in all circumstances.*

1 Thessalonians 5:18

# BE THANKFUL FOR NO TIGERS

The Sundarbans is a vast, swampy jungle in Bangladesh where the Ganges and Brahmaputra rivers join in emptying into the Indian Ocean. Besides living in one of the poorest nations on earth, the people of the Sundarbans have even greater worries—their land is full of man-eating tigers!

Ranga, a young man living in the Sundarbans, lost a dozen members of his extended family to attacks by tigers. Ranga is deathly scared to venture out on jungle paths hunting for the food his family so badly needs, but he must. As a devout Muslim he thanks Allah that his life has been spared a horrible death by a hungry tiger, and he holds onto the certainty that God will protect him.

If Ranga can trust so completely, so can you. Give thanks and be grateful that although you'll certainly face difficulties and fears in life, God is there with you, protecting you through it all.

Steven Cole

The Lord is my strength
and my shield... I will give thanks
to him in song.

Psalm 28:7

# GRATITUDE IS GOOD FOR YOU!

A group of psychologists recently conducted a research project on gratitude and thankfulness. They divided participants into three groups. People in the first group practiced daily gratitude exercises like keeping a list of things for which they were grateful. They reported higher levels of alertness, enthusiasm, determination, optimism, and energy. They also experienced less depression and stress than the control group. Unsurprisingly, they were also a lot happier than the group of participants who were directed to keep a daily journal of all the bad things that happened to them each day.

One of the psychologists concluded that anyone can increase their sense of well-being and create positive social effects just from counting their blessings.

Ellen Vaughn

# THREE PLACES TO EAT

"Three places to eat!" the Dutch visitor exclaimed upon seeing the home of his American cousin. The wide-eyed Hollander could scarcely believe he was seeing a breakfast room, a formal dining room and a porch with table and chairs. Another visitor, a just-returned Peace Corps volunteer, said the walk-in closet would be a bedroom in the Dominican Republic where she had served. Another visitor from Hong Kong said the house would cost eight times as much in his homeland and would certainly not come with a huge lot. And yet the house was small by American standards.

In our prayers most of us thank God for plentiful food, good health, a child on the honor roll and similar blessings. But as you look at your daily life, be thankful for everything—even what you might see as your simple home.

Steven Cole

*Let us be thankful.*

Hebrews 12:28

I thank and praise you,
O God of my fathers.

Daniel 2:23

# DELIGHT IN IMPERFECT GIFTS

Did you ever go to an outlet store where they sell products labeled "slightly imperfect?" Sometimes the imperfections are easily seen, other times they are barely noticeable. The same is true in our lives, not only with the products we buy but with the gifts we receive.

We must learn to be grateful for all the "slightly imperfect" gifts. If we withhold our gratitude in hopes of receiving the perfect spouse, child, body, or birthday present, we would never be grateful at all.

God himself chooses to delight in imperfect gifts—in you and me. Even though our hearts are flawed and shadowed, even though we give them tentatively and with mixed motives, he receives them with unspeakable joy. Heaven itself rejoices at the gift of one repentant sinner's heart.

John Ortberg

"Serve the food."

Genesis 43:31

# SUPERBOWL SPREAD

A supermarket chain ran an ad reminding people to stock up on enough food to last until the end of the Superbowl game. The accompanying photograph showed a big screen TV and fans seated around a large coffee table laden with bowl upon bowl of nuts, crackers, chips, dips, cheeses, meatballs, and cocktail sausages. A small boy knelt beside the table with wide-open mouth about to receive an enormous slice of pizza.

Besides promoting unhealthy eating habits the ad also promoted disregard for God's blessing of ample food. In a world where many people go to bed hungry God does not want those of us who can afford to eat well to overeat every chance we get. He wants us to be grateful for the bounty he provides, to partake in moderation and savor the blessing.

Steven Cole

## DISGUISED BLESSINGS

Remember that God often works through other people. When you start asking God to meet your needs, you may find that he doesn't always do it in the way you expected. You may think he is going to change someone, like your spouse, your friend, or your boss, so that he or she will meet your need. It may be, however, that someone else comes along to listen or meet one of our desires. Our experience, when we look back over our lives, is that we can see ways in which God brought people into our lives to meet our needs in ways we never imagined.

Mark and Debra Laaser

To the wicked, God says: ... "He who sacrifices thank offerings honors me, and he prepares the way so that I may show him the salvation of God."

Psalm 50:16, 23

I will lie down and sleep in peace, for you alone, O Lord, make me dwell in safety.

Psalm 4:8

# A CLOSE CALL

Stan and Brenda had gone to their favorite restaurant for their anniversary. When they emerged it was dark and snowing hard so driving was treacherous. Slowly they picked their way toward home. As they approached a stop sign and slowed, a car came speeding into the intersection from the side road and slid out of control into the path of their car. Just as suddenly, the out-of-control car careened narrowly past them, knocked down the stop sign and landed in a ditch.

Seeing that the other driver was unhurt, Stan and Brenda went on, complaining angrily all the way home about the "stupid" person speeding on an icy road. "Probably drunk!" Brenda snorted. It was only when safely home that Brenda and Stan realized they had to let go of their anger and be grateful for being alive.

Steven Cole

# EACH DAY IS A GIFT

Try getting up before daybreak. See the dawn emerge like a chorus in the morning twilight. You'll hear it whisper, "Today is a gift for you." As you watch for that soaring burst of the sun, let the serene beauty of that simple moment be stored in your soul.

Each time the sun peeks above the horizon, it brings a fresh promise—the gift of another day. Greet the day by beginning it well.

Develop a routine for getting up in the morning—your personally designed "order of the day." Wake up a little early, brew a special cup of tea or flavored coffee, and before it gets hectic, spend a few moments in anticipation of what this day might bring. Seek the quiet comfort of a renewed heart and be thankful for the gift of today.

Anonymous

Let us come before him with thanksgiving.

Psalm 95:2

## A GRATEFUL HEART

Sometimes things go wrong all day—your computer freezes up during an important project, you get a flat tire when you're running late, the washing machine snaps a belt when it's full of wet towels. It's easy to lose perspective at times like these. It's easy to see more rain than rainbow.

But take a few moments to think of some things you can give thanks for. Remind yourself that you have been given an abundance of blessings that enrich, brighten and sweeten your life. Then tell others how thankful you are. See how many hearts you can lift and smiles you can elicit.

Anonymous

God has scattered abroad
his gifts to the poor.

2 Corinthians 9:9

Jesus said, "Everyone who asks receives; he who seeks finds; and to him who knocks, the door will be opened."

Luke 11:10

## USING GIFTS

Everybody receives a gift. We are all called by God. We are all equipped and expected to contribute. Every gift is chosen by the Master. We may like our gift, or we may not. We may torture ourselves by desiring what belongs to another, but it will do us no good. No one decides on his or her giftedness.

God has been very generous. There are no no-talent people in the world. Not only that, God offers to partner with you in your life. He offers to guide you when you need wisdom, encourage you when you falter, pick you up when you sink, and forgive you when you stray. He offers us himself as the best gift of all. Be grateful.

John Ortberg

## BE GRATEFUL THAT ALL ARE GRACED

Martin Luther said, "God lets rain fall on both the thankful and the unthankful. He gives money, property and all types of things from the earth to the very worst scoundrels. Why does he do this? He does it out of genuine, pure love. His heart is full and overflowing with love. He pours his love over everyone, leaving no one out, whether good or bad, worthy or unworthy. This love is righteous, godly, whole and complete. It doesn't single out certain people or separate people into groups. He freely gives his love to all."

If you have sinned, repent, take heart and be grateful for God's blessing and love.

John Ortberg

Jesus said,
"Blessed are you who hunger now,
for you will be satisfied."

Luke 6:21

We have had enough to eat
and plenty to spare, because the Lord
has blessed his people.

2 Chronicles 31:10

# THE OTHER WORLD

In many third world countries civil strife is a fact of daily life. Go to the store and you might be blown to bits by a fanatic. There's not enough to eat and no jobs to earn enough to buy food. There's no government you can count on, no system of fair and just laws, no stable currency, no health care, no protection from thieves or bullies, no place to run and no place to hide, no freedom, no democracy.

We often have a tendency to give thanks only for the extras that are beyond the basics. We need to realize that the things many of us take for granted not only can't be taken for granted in the Third World, they often don't exist at all. In your prayers today, give thanks to God for the basics of daily life that you enjoy.

Steven Cole

*After waiting patiently Abraham received what was promised.*

Hebrews 6:15

# AN AGONIZING WAIT

Bryan had chosen the wrong wife and she had chosen the wrong husband for her. The couple divorced and Bryan assumed it wouldn't be long before Miss Right came along because, after all, it was what he was praying for. Little did he know that he faced sixteen years of loneliness, endless nights spent at singles functions and many disappointing short-term relationships. In what he thought was the end, he gave up looking for love.

But then a friend introduced him to Sarah. Within months his prayers were finally answered. They were hopelessly in love and soon to be married. Now, with each passing year, Bryan becomes more and more grateful to God for answering his prayers and bringing him a beautiful wife—his soul mate. He now knows an agonizing wait doesn't mean God has turned a deaf ear. Often God's timing just isn't our timing.

Steven Cole

# TWO SIDES OF A COIN

Gratitude toward God is the corollary of faith in God. When we have faith, we affirm explicitly that we are recipients of God's favors, and implicitly we recognize and affirm God as the giver. When we are grateful, we recognize and honor God explicitly as the giver, and we implicitly recognize and affirm ourselves as recipients of God's gift. In a way, faith and gratitude are two sides of the same coin. At the same time, there is a certain progression from faith to gratitude. Faith receives God's gifts as gifts; gratitude receives them well.

Miroslav Volf

Have faith in the Lord your God.

2 Chronicles 20:20

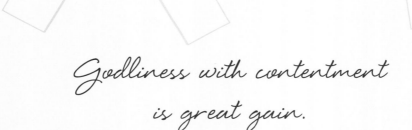

*Godliness with contentment*
*is great gain.*

1 Timothy 6:6

## VALUE WHAT GOD VALUES

The ability to assign value is one of the rarest and greatest gifts in the world.

So value what God values. There is an ancient story about a poor traveler who is amazed by the welcome he receives at a monastery. He is served a lavish meal, escorted to their finest room, and given a new set of clothes to replace the rags he arrived in. Before leaving, he commented to the abbot on how well he was treated. Yes, the abbot said, we always treat our guests as if they were angels—just to be on the safe side.

John Ortberg

*Sacrifice thank offerings to God,*
*fulfill your vows to the Most High.*

Psalm 50:14

# THE DANGER OF INGRATITUDE

One of the primary dangers of ingratitude is that it's contagious. It is striking to see how destructive the writers of Scripture believe ingratitude is. It is one of our most ragged qualities.

Art critic Robert Hughes wrote a penetrating critique of American society a few years ago, *The Culture of Complaint*. His thesis is that we live in a society where people perceive themselves to be entitled to having all desires fulfilled. We take this to be part of our birthright. We accord ourselves victim status when it doesn't happen. We live in the culture of complaint. It forms our minds and hearts.

John Ortberg

# GO DUTCH

Recent findings reveal that two-thirds of Americans are overweight, and many are grossly fat. A young man visiting from The Netherlands couldn't believe his eyes, because in his country you rarely see anyone fat. In fact, when he e-mailed his friends back home they thought he was exaggerating about American obesity. So the young man went to a shopping mall and took pictures of the throngs of people waddling along with a big drink in one hand and a snack in the other to prove he was telling the truth.

In his country, as in much of Europe, people do not eat mindlessly. For example, the Dutch take several coffee breaks each day. The cups are small and the coffee, perhaps accompanied by a cookie, is lingered over and savored—a grateful tribute to the bounty God has provided.

It's important to appreciate and be thankful for the blessing of food. We don't show gratitude if we abuse our blessings.

Steven Cole

You will have plenty to eat, until you are full, and you will praise the name of the Lord your God.

Joel 2:26

## SHELVES OF ACHIEVEMENT

If you walked into my office, you would probably notice the baseballs on my shelf. Each one commemorates a special achievement from my baseball career, but there are two I prize more highly than the rest. The first is the ball from my best pitching performance in the major leagues. The other is the ball that I hit out of the park from my first home run in the majors.

Just because I could no longer play the game, I didn't take the baseballs off my shelf. I prize the memories and achievements they represent. I'm encouraged to know that there are shelves yet to be filled in my future, just as there are in yours. God alone knows what could end up on our shelves!

Dave Dravecky

"My people will be filled with my bounty," declares the Lord.

Jeremiah 31:14

Sing to the Lord a new song,
for he has done marvelous things.

Psalm 98:1

# MAN'S BEST FRIEND

There is no more grateful a creature than a dog. A dog will happily gobble up and relish any food you set before him (unlike a cat). A dog will contently sleep in whatever place you provide, whether the room is warm or cold and whether the surface is soft or hard. A dog will be glad to see you when you come home regardless of how grumpy you might be. A dog will love any master who treats him well. A dog never complains. A dog always forgives.

Perhaps God created dogs to provide a lesson. Take a clue from dogs—happiness and contentment are right under your nose.

Steven Cole

# THE "THANK YOU" CONNECTION

It's incredible: The small, compliant human action of saying "thank you" constantly links us to the awesome Creator of the universe. In the practice of perceiving every part of every day as a gift from him, we stay connected to Christ. We can't wander away, as our hearts are so prone to do. As we thank God for his presents, we remain in his presence. He says, "You are welcome." And more. We begin to see things from his point of view. The conversations of a continually grateful heart become a way of life, a fountain flowing in us, the means by which we acknowledge our dependence on Christ, enjoy him lavishly, and run to do whatever he wants.

Ellen Vaughn

Give thanks to the Lord, for he is good.

Psalm 107:1

*Your generosity will result in thanksgiving to God.*

2 Corinthians 9:11

# BROCCOLI, UGH!

I want to find a zillion things to be thankful for today. One little girl was overjoyed one Thanksgiving Day because broccoli wasn't on the table! When God does make broccoli part of the menu, I've learned it's only because he has a greater good in mind.

What are you thankful for right this very moment? Start today by being grateful for the tiniest things—water to drink, a moment to rest, the color of a flower or sunset, a song on the radio. Keep looking for sights, smells, and sounds that make you feel pleasure. And something else to be thankful for? The fact that you are here to be thankful!

Barbara Johnson

There are different kinds of working,
but the same God works all
of them in all men.

1 Corinthians 12:6

# BE THANKFUL THERE'S MARV

Marv's job was to clean the portable toilets used at outdoor events. He was conscientious and worked hard, and his boss noticed. So, one day Marv was offered a promotion to driver of the truck that transported the toilets. But Marv didn't want the promotion. He liked cleaning toilets because it was mindless work and there was no one breathing down his neck. Not daring to confront his boss, Marv asked his pastor to intervene. Puzzled, the pastor talked to Marv's boss and assured him Marv was happiest continuing to clean toilets.

Marv was grateful for a job that suited him. Marv's boss was grateful for a hard-working employee. And Marv's pastor was grateful he could help. Be grateful there are people like Marv who are willing to do a job few others would want.

Steven Cole

# FUSS WITH THE FLOWERS

I chuckle when I get to look into the face of a smiling pansy. I'm so amazed at how God has cleverly, humorously, and beautifully designed this world. Pansies are the chortlers of the garden. Other varieties are joyful and know how to celebrate—the trumpeting lily, for example—but the little pansies are crowded close to the earth giggling their heads off. Sometimes I stick my face down by theirs to be a part of the fun for a moment.

Want simple pleasures? Take time to fuss with the flowers.

Patsy Clairmont

*Always give thanks to God the Father
for everything.*

Ephesians 5:20

*I will give thanks to the Lord
because of his righteousness.*

Psalm 7:17

# THANK YOU, JESUS

The prayers I find myself saying most often are, "Be with me" and "Thank you, Jesus." In Flannery O'Connor's short story "Resurrection," Mrs. Turbin is always saying, "Thank you, Jesus. Thank you, Jesus." There's something about the sound of that phrase that is musical and lyric. It has a nice rhythm. I say it probably a hundred times a day.

Marilyn Meberg

*With praise and thanksgiving they sang to the Lord.*

Ezra 3:11

# GRACIOUS GRATITUDE

In his classic *Religious Affections*, Jonathon Edwards called the fundamental, primary form of thankfulness "gracious gratitude." It gives thanks for who God is. It gives thanks for his character—his goodness, love, power, excellencies—regardless of any favors received. It is the real evidence of the Holy Spirit in a person's life.

Ellen Vaughn

# BRINGING UP YOUR PARENTS

Mark Twain once said something like, "When I was fourteen my father was so stupid I could hardly bear him. But by the time I was twenty-one I was so amazed at how much he had learned in seven years." Often it is only in hindsight that we can give our folks the honor and respect for the influence they have had on our lives. While they are far from perfect, they deserve our gratitude.

I was thirty years old before I told my parents how grateful I am for them. What have you always wanted to say to honor your folks? Say it soon, before it's too late.

Duncan Banks

Honor your father and mother, so that you may live long in the land the Lord your God is giving you.

Exodus 20:12

The Lord is my shepherd,
I shall not be in want.

Psalm 23:1

# SHEEP AREN'T SO DUMB

Sheep, down through the ages, have had bad press. We think of them as stubborn and stupid. But sheep know what's good for them. The shepherd leads the sheep to food and water, and the sheep know what to do.

How often do we resist the God who leads us to food, shelter, refreshment and rest? How many of our difficulties result from our stubborn refusal to accept these good gifts? What God intends as refreshment, we shirk as duty. What he offers as rest, we misinterpret as restriction. Failing to see, or to trust, the good pastures to which he is leading us, we invent an endless list of other "needs" and press blindly for their fulfillment. We need eyes to see the perfect provision he has made for us in the place in which we stand.

Gerard Kelly

Jesus said, "Father, I thank you that you have heard me."

John 11:41

*I have learned to be content whatever the circumstances.*

Philippians 4:11

## GIVE THANKS FOR THE SCRAPS

Most of us don't have to stop and think about where our dinner will come from. It will be there for us every day, and that's just part of life. Aren't we fortunate? But for people in the Third World the next bite of food is not a given.

An aid worker in Sudan, who was helping people caught in a terrible famine, tells the story of a woman he saw gathering scraps from a rubbish heap. Before she and her children ate the meager meal she bowed her head and thanked God for the food.

Roz Stirling

Jesus said, "When you pray, say:
Give us each day our daily bread."

Luke 11:2-3

## UNIVERSAL GRATITUDE

Habitual gratitude is not unique to Christianity. Buddhism, Hinduism, and Islam commend thankfulness as a morally beneficial state that produces reciprocal kindnesses. The Koran also teaches that true gratitude draws more blessings upon the believer, as in Allah's promise, "If you are grateful, I will give you more."

Ellen Vaughn

When times are good, be happy;
but when times are bad, consider:
God has made the one as well
as the other.

Ecclesiastes 7:14

*The gift of God is eternal life.*

Romans 6:23

# DELAYING GRATIFICATION

The ability to wait well is a test of maturity. Psychologists speak of this as the ability to endure delayed gratification. M. Scott Peck writes, "Delaying gratification is a process of scheduling the pain and pleasure of life in such a way as to enhance the pleasure by meeting and experiencing the pain first and getting it over with. It is the only decent way to live."

John Ortberg

# CELEBRATE YOUR FEELINGS

It's pretty common to appreciate and give thanks for things, such as the new camera you've been wanting, or events, such as your son earning the rank of Eagle Scout. But how often do we pause to give thanks for our emotions, our feelings, the thoughts in our head that touch us deeply?

My wife was watching a winter sunset from her sewing room window recently when she called me to come view the scene with her. I was touched. What feelings must rise up in her heart upon seeing God's handiwork? What feelings of love did she experience that she wanted to share something simple, yet special to her, with me? At times like this I am grateful for her presence and the thought of her thoughts.

Steven Cole

The Lord knows the thoughts of man.

Psalm 94:11

Give thanks to the God of gods.

Psalm 136: 2

## JUST SAY THANK YOU

There is an art to saying thank you. Start by just saying it. Make a list of people you need to thank, then write them a note. If you don't know what to say, take a clue from Paul and be specific. "It was good of you to share in my troubles," he said (Philippians 4:14).

Has anyone written you a timely letter when you were in trouble? Have they shared in your troubles? In what way? Sit down and think about the help you received and write a letter, send an e-mail, pick up the phone, or pay a visit. Just say thank you.

Jill Briscoe

*All hard work brings a profit.*

Proverbs 14:23

## YOU DESERVE A BREAK

The purpose of our existence is to love and enjoy God forever. Whatever furthers that purpose is, to that very extent, good. Whatever does not further that purpose must be—however reluctantly—let go. One of these good things is pleasurable idleness. You deserve a break today—maybe more than one. Take it as gladly and gratefully as you can, and then remember to share the joy.

David and Lo-Ann Trembley

# A SLIPPERY SLOPE

Ungratefulness—the refusal to glorify and thank God—is the clearest manifestation of the mother sin, human rebellion against God. It opens the gate to a slippery slope where God lets us go. How do we make sure we don't slide down that slimy path? First, it's important to understand that a grateful heart is a gift of grace. God can make gratitude flow powerfully in our lives, like a fountain. It is actually irrepressible for those who realize that they have been rescued from torture and death—for no other reason than the undeserved kindness of God.

Ellen Vaughn

Therefore their path will become slippery.

Jeremiah 23:12

*My lover is mine and I am his.*

Song of Songs 2:16

# THANK GOD FOR YOUR PARTNER

Never-married, divorced and widowed people often profess publicly that they are contented with the single life. But privately, to friends, they more often speak of their loneliness and their strong desire to find a partner. But even with numerous places to meet people—church, work, school—and websites that promise to match men and women according to compatibility, it's a frustrating task to find Mr. or Miss Right.

All married couples nag and fight on occasion, and it's tempting to think of finding a better match. But unless your partner totally ignores you or, worse yet, abuses you, stick it out and be grateful that you have someone with whom to share your life. Think of your partner's good points, and express your appreciation for having him or her in your life. Because you really might not like being single.

Steven Cole

Excerpts contained in this book were pulled from the following resources:

Banks, Duncan. *Breakfast with God Volume 1*. Grand Rapids: Zondervan, 2000.

Briscoe, Jill. *Spiritual Arts*. Grand Rapids: Zondervan, 2007.

_____. *Joy for a Woman's Soul*. Grand Rapids: Zondervan, 1998.

Kelly, Gerard. *Breakfast with God Volume 2*. Grand Rapids: Zondervan, 2000.

Laaser, Mark and Debra. *The Seven Desires of Every Heart*. Grand Rapids: Zondervan, 2008.

Ortberg, John. *Everybody's Normal Till You Get to Know Them*. Grand Rapids: Zondervan, 2003.

Ortberg, John. *If You Want to Walk on Water, You've Got to Get Out of the Boat*. Grand Rapids: Zondervan, 2001.

Ortberg, John. *Living the God Life*. Grand Rapids: Zondervan, 2004.

Ortberg, John. *Love Beyond Reason*. Grand Rapids: Zondervan, 1998.

_____. *Simple Gifts: Unwrapping the Special Moments of Everyday Life*. Grand Rapids: Zondervan, 1999.

_____. *Soul Retreats for Women*. Grand Rapids: Zondervan, 2002.

Stirling, Roz. *Breakfast with God Volume 3*. Grand Rapids: Zondervan, 2000.

_____. *Stories of Hope for a Healthy Soul*. Grand Rapids: Zondervan, 1999.

Trembley, David and Lo-Ann. *The Gratitude Attitude*. Grand Rapids: Zondervan, 2003.

Vaughn, Ellen. *Radical Gratitude*. Grand Rapids: Zondervan, 2005.

Volf, Miroslav. *Free of Charge*. Grand Rapids: Zondervan, 2005.